THE CREATIVE CURRICULUM®
LearningGames®

24–36 Months

Joseph Sparling and Isabelle Lewis

Foreword by Diane Trister Dodge

Teaching Strategies Inc.

Washington, DC

This book of *LearningGames* is being shared with the family of

_____

Editor: Kai-leé Berke
Design: Carla Uriona
Layout/production: Tony MacFarlane and Abner Nieves

Published by:
Teaching Strategies, Inc.
P.O. Box 42243
Washington, DC 20015
www.TeachingStrategies.com

ISBN: 978-1-933021-60-7

Printed and bound in the United States of America

2012	2011	2010	2009	2008	2007
6	5	4	3	2	1

Contents

THE CREATIVE CURRICULUM®
LearningGames®

Foreword

Dear Parents,

It gives me great pleasure to introduce you to an exciting program called *The Creative Curriculum® LearningGames®*. The games are designed to build the kinds of skills that lead to successful, lifelong learning for your child. You are the key to making this happen.

On a regular basis you will be receiving a colorful handout describing simple and fun games to play with your child. They don't require any special toys or materials. You can do them as part of your everyday experiences with your child. But they can make a big difference, and they already have made a difference for thousands of children and families.

There are five different sets of *LearningGames* for children of different ages. You will receive only the games appropriate for your child. It's never too soon to start. Right from birth, your child is learning and growing. The experiences you provide during the first 5 years of life will help to build your child's brain, develop thinking skills, promote social skills, and build your child's confidence as a learner.

You are your child's first and most important teacher. Everything you do with your child, everything you say, every song you sing, and every object you give your child to play with teach important lessons. One of the wonderful results of using these games is that they help you to build a positive relationship with your child. And as your child is learning, you are as well. You will gain an understanding of child development and many practical ideas for guiding your child's learning.

Many programs using the *LearningGames* are also implementing either *The Creative Curriculum® for Infants, Toddlers & Twos* or *The Creative Curriculum® for Preschool*. As the lead author on these comprehensive curriculum materials, I am very excited to be able to offer this parent component, too. Children benefit the most when the important adults in their lives—their parents, caregivers, teachers, health care specialists, or home visitors—are working together to support their learning and growth.

I wish you great enjoyment and success,

Diane Trister Dodge
President
Teaching Strategies, Inc.

THE CREATIVE CURRICULUM®
LearningGames®

Acknowledgments

Many people helped in the preparation of *The Creative Curriculum* *LearningGames*. We would like to thank Kai-leé Berke and Heather Baker for their thoughtful writing contributions and for finding wonderful children's books that enhance each game. Thank you to Nancy Guadagno, Sharon Samber, Toni Bickart, and Rachel Tickner, our editors, for their attention to detail. We appreciate the work of Carla Uriona, who designed the new format for the activities, and Abner Nieves and Tony MacFarlane for their careful layout work. Thanks to Nancy Guadagno and Kai-leé Berke for their patience and persistence in moving the writing, editing, and production process forward.

Checklist for
The Creative Curriculum® LearningGames®:
24-36 months

I have shared the LearningGames *checked below with the family of* _____

Given to Family	LearningGames Activity Number and Title	Date Given to Family/Notes
☐	68. Toys Peeking Out	
☐	69. Create a Face	
☐	70. Family Circle Games	
☐	71. Dress-Up Play	
☐	72. Me in a Mirror	
☐	73. See It a New Way	
☐	74. What's Your Name?	
☐	75. Sharing Nursery Rhymes	
☐	76. Show One and Two	
☐	77. Color Sorting	
☐	78. Building Blocks	
☐	79. Others Have Needs, Too	
☐	80. Making Os and Xs	
☐	81. Play With Others	
☐	82. Choose the Doll's Clothes	
☐	83. Drawing Around Things	

Given to Family	*LearningGames* Activity Number and Title	Date Given to Family/Notes
☐	84. Using a Different Voice	
☐	85. Happy Face, Sad Face	
☐	86. Two Together	
☐	87. Choosing and Stringing	
☐	88. In, Out, and Around	
☐	89. Giving One to Each	
☐	90. A Fun Path	
☐	91. Words for Time	
☐	92. Listen and Support	
☐	93. Pair and Sort Pictures	
☐	94. What's Gone?	
☐	95. Cut and Paste	
☐	96. Help Him Help Himself	
☐	97. What Would Happen If…?	
☐	98. Run and Walk Together	
☐	99. Tell Family Stories	
☐	100. I See Something That Is…	

What Your Child May Be Doing
Two-Year-Olds (24–36 Months)

Social/Emotional Development

Have strong feelings and may use actions instead of words to express their emotions

Begin to learn about taking turns but should not be expected to share toys and materials

Interact with other children for longer periods

Engage in simple pretend play

Begin to use caring behaviors to help and comfort others

Use toys (balls, blocks, lotto games) with other people

Cognitive Development

Want to do things by themselves

Enjoy sensory toys with various sounds and textures

Sort and match objects and pictures by size, color, or shape

Experiment to see what will happen as a result of their actions

Complete puzzles with a few pieces

Make sounds with musical instruments

Physical Development

Develop small muscle skills, such as turning pages, pouring, opening containers, and using scissors

Stack and build with blocks

Begin to coordinate eye and hand movements (for example, threading beads on laces, manipulating snaps and zippers)

Walk well, tiptoe, and learn to run

Begin to gain large muscle skills, such as throwing, catching, kicking, jumping, and hopping

Pull and push things, such as boxes, doll carriages, and other wheeled toys

Sit on and use their feet to propel riding toys

Language and Literacy Development

Talk in simple sentences that gradually increase from two to several words

Increase their ability to listen and to speak

Engage in conversation and ask questions

Begin to make sense of basic time concepts (for example, before and after)

Enjoy books with rhymes and predictable words they can anticipate and repeat

Tell very simple stories

Begin to express feelings with words

Toys Peeking Out

What could this be?

Can you find the doll?

Encourage your child to identify a toy by seeing just one part of it.

This requires your child to notice identifying characteristics and then remember the whole object.

THE
CREATIVE CURRICULUM®
LearningGames®
Copyright 2007 Joseph Sparling

Why this is important

Recognizing part of an object requires your child to remember the whole object. This process is called visual closure. Visual closure is used in many tasks in life, including reading. When she can say the name of the hidden object, she is expressing what she knows using her growing vocabulary.

What you do

- Show your child one familiar toy covered with a towel. Make sure a part of the toy, like the wheel on a truck, can still be seen. Let your child uncover the toy and play with it.

- Make the game harder by partially covering two different objects such as a doll and a toy car. Hide them under the towel and ask your child to find the doll. *Do you know where the doll is? Can you find it for me?*

- If she does not see the doll, uncover more of it to make it easier to find. Repeat the game until she can easily locate each item.

- Invite your child to use language during the game. As she chooses an object, ask her to name it before she takes it from its hiding place. *Can you tell me what you found? If she doesn't know the name of the toy, offer help. You found the doll! Can you say doll?*

- Give her time to play with the toy before repeating the game.

Ready to move on?

Add more toys to the game so that she has a few more to choose from. You can also add toys or household items that are less familiar to her and therefore harder to recognize.

Let's read together!

Hide and Snake
by Keith Baker

Create a Face

And now you're giving her a nose.

Talk about the parts of a face as your child creates one using different shapes.

Your child's self-image will strengthen as she learns how to create a likeness of herself.

Why this is important

From their earliest days, tiny babies recognize a circle with two eyes and a mouth as a face. Now your child can practice creating her own representation of a face. Using shapes to represent parts of the face helps her learn the correct places for eyes, mouth, and nose. As she gains experience making a representation of a face, she shows that she understands parts of herself and strengthens her self-image.

What you do

- Cut out a large paper circle and a variety of smaller circles or other shapes, and give them to your child.

- Point to the big circle and say: *Let's make a face together. What will it need to see with?* You can suggest some shapes if she needs help.

- Ask what the face needs to eat with. Let her think about what is needed before telling her.

- Offer your child a mirror so she can review the parts of her face. Point out that her eyes are above her mouth and the nose is in the middle.

- Do not change the face your child creates, even if it is incorrect. She will eventually learn where each part belongs.

Another idea

Think of other opportunities to create faces together. You can draw faces with crayons or finger paints. Playing with sand or play dough also offer chances to make simple faces together.

Let's read together!

The Wide-Mouthed Frog
by Keith Faulkner

Family Circle Games

Ring around the Rosie!

Invite your child to join in a family game.

Having fun in a group helps your child feel loved and supported by his family.

THE
CREATIVE CURRICULUM®
Learning Games®

Copyright 2007 Joseph Sparling

Why this is important

Your child will learn how to get along in the world as he participates in activities with family or a group of friends. Feeling secure in a warm and loving group helps your child get ready to try new games. As he feels encouraged to participate, he will trust his own abilities to contribute to a group. Group activities help him learn how to interact with and be more confident with adults and his peers.

What you do

- Make time in your day to play games with your child and other family members or friends.

- Play simple group games such as "Ring Around the Rosie" or "Duck, Duck, Goose". When singing or listening to music, form a band and invite the whole family or group to participate. Give each member a pan and spoon to bang with, or use whistles, bells, or horns.

- Invite each family member to make up a silly dance for the others to try. Hold hands with your child as you dance together. *Watch me hop around the circle. Can you hop, too?*

- Give your child a chance to invent a game for everyone to play together.

- Use family time as an opportunity to share love and support.

Another idea

Think of other parts of the day that can be spent together as a family. Family activities can include meal times, art projects, travel games, and quiet time reading together.

Let's read together!

I Like It When
by Mary Murphy

Dress-Up Play

You chose a hat with flowers.

Talk positively to your child about her choices during dress-up play.

Dress-up play offers your child a chance to choose for herself and develop her imagination.

THE CREATIVE CURRICULUM®
LearningGames®

Why this is important

Most children enjoy trying out various kinds of clothes and seeing themselves in new ways. In this game, your child can decide and choose for herself how to dress up. A child who feels good about herself because her decisions have been accepted will have a more positive attitude in her approach to other people.

What you do

- Give your child a box of simple dress-up clothes and accessories such as hats, gloves, shoes, etc. Make sure your child has a mirror nearby while playing.

- Encourage your child to choose a few items to wear. Talk about the items she chooses. *You are wearing Daddy's red hat! It looks nice with your blue shoes.*

- Keep your comments positive and encouraging as your child decides what to wear on her own.

- Remember that both boys and girls will enjoy this activity. Dress-up play provides your child the chance to experiment freely with various roles without embarrassment.

- Change the items in the box periodically to keep your child's interest, but remember that simple items, such as shoes, scarves, and hats, work well.

Another idea

Expand dress-up time to allow your child to wear her new outfit all day if she wants. Let her know that you value her choices.

Let's read together!

Hats
by Debbie Bailey

Me in a Mirror

Look at you!

Talk to your child about what she sees as she discovers herself in the mirror.

Watching herself in the mirror helps your child connect what she sees with what she feels her body doing.

Why this is important

Your child may enjoy examining herself in front of a mirror. Practicing smiles, making faces, brushing her teeth, or washing her face all help her connect what she sees in the mirror with what she feels her body doing. The more your child learns about herself and what she can do, the more comfortable she will feel in new situations.

What you do

- Give your child a safe, hand-held mirror. **Unless it is a toy made of unbreakable Plexiglas®, you need to stay right next to her to make sure the mirror doesn't break.**

- Encourage her to make faces. *Can you stick out your tongue?*

- Offer her a comb, toothbrush, or washcloth and let her play with them as she watches herself.

- Describe her actions as she sees them in the mirror. *You're washing your nose. The comb is getting caught in your hair!* Make sure you let her direct her own play.

- Use a wall mirror to allow your child to see her whole body. She may pose or dance in front of it. You can join her and talk about her image, but give her time to play on her own.

Another idea

Keep your child's interest in the mirror by offering hats, scarves, or jewelry for her to try on.

Let's read together!

Mirror Mirror What Will I Be?
by Christopher Inns

See It a New Way

Oh, look at this big rock.

Give your child a plastic magnifying glass, show him how to use it, and talk with him about his discoveries.

Using a magnifying glass lets your child see ordinary objects in a new way and increases his curiosity about the world.

THE CREATIVE CURRICULUM®
LearningGames®

Copyright 2007 Joseph Sparling

Why this is important

Giving your child a magnifying glass helps him discover a new way to look at the world around him. He will discover how the magnifier makes familiar objects look different. With many experiences, he will remember the object as it was and learn how it can look differently.

What you do

- Give your child a plastic magnifying glass and invite him to examine and explore with it.

- Make sure he has a few objects handy to explore. Talk about the differences he notices, using words like *big* and *different*. **Supervise closely when your child handles tiny objects. Watch carefully to make sure your child does not put any small objects in his mouth.**

- Answer his questions and respond with enthusiasm as he shares his discoveries with you. *Wow! There are so many tiny spots on the leaf!*

- Notice how he looks at an object, such as a flower, and then views it with the magnifier. He may take the glass away, look again, and then look one more time through the glass.

Another idea

Let him use the magnifying glass to look at the food on his plate before he eats, or take the magnifying glass with you when you go on a walk together or go to the grocery store. You can offer him another interesting view of the world by using sunglasses or plastic colored lenses.

Let's read together!

Baby Food
by Saxton Freymann

What's Your Name?

I see Edna Smith.

Use your child's name in songs, stories, and games to encourage her to say it.

Recognizing and remembering her name helps your child strengthen her self-image.

THE
CREATIVE CURRICULUM®
LearningGames®

Why this is important

A young child may quickly learn to recognize her name, but she may have few opportunities to speak her name. Giving your child practice saying and using her full name and encouraging her to look carefully at her written name develops her sense of identity.

What you do

- Begin by speaking your child's name clearly so that she can learn it and recognize it when others speak it.

- Introduce your child to others using her full name. Occasionally use her full name when speaking to her: *Thank you, Shawna Johnson.*

- Make up rhymes or simple songs using her name. *Maria, Maria, I love you. Maria, Maria, touch your shoe.*

- Make up games that require your child to say her name. She can knock on the door as you ask, *Who is it?*

Let's read together!

A Bit More Bert
by Allan Ahlberg

Ready to move on?

Sit together and look at family photos. Name each person you see. You can include written labels for each person as a way to help her learn to recognize her written name and the names of others.

Sharing Nursery Rhymes

One shoe off and one shoe on…

Teach your child some of the nursery rhymes you learned when you were young.

Sharing songs from your childhood can help your child learn more about her family's culture.

THE CREATIVE CURRICULUM®
LearningGames®

Why this is important

Reciting rhymes with your child provides an excellent opportunity to teach her about the rhythm in language. Using the language and traditional rhymes of your childhood and your family's culture helps your child feel included in a group. Songs and stories are things that many people share in common.

What you do

- Sing your favorite nursery rhymes from your childhood to your child. Make sure to include the favorite nursery rhymes of your family's culture.

- Invite your child to repeat short, simple rhymes. At first she may yell out just a few words that sound alike, but as time goes on she will learn to say more of the words.

- Chant the rhyme to add rhythm. Clap to the beat as you say the words.

Another idea

Invite your child to act out a favorite nursery rhyme. Join in the acting, but let her be the leader.

Let's read together!

Hickory, Dickory, Dock: And Other Favorite Nursery Rhymes by Sanja Rescek

Show One and Two

Yes, that plate has two.

With your child create and talk about groups made up of one, two, or many items.

Your child will gradually begin to understand that one, two, and other numbers mean a particular amount.

Why this is important

Helping your child say and use number words strengthens his understanding of the number concepts of *one* and *two*. Grouping objects helps your child see relationships and make comparisons. With practice he may learn that *one* is different from *many*. As he grows he will begin to make more complicated judgments, such as the difference between *a few* and *many*.

What you do

- Look for occasions when you can talk about *one* and *more than one* with your child.

- Invite your child to play a game with you. Group objects such as small blocks or crackers in bowls or stack them on the table.

- Talk to your child about the groups. *See, this bowl has one cracker. This bowl has many.*

- Ask your child to show you the bowl with one cracker. Respond enthusiastically when he chooses correctly. *You chose the bowl with one!*

- Change the game to finding two, after he feels comfortable finding one object.

- Look for objects around the house that come in pairs such as socks, shoes, and gloves. Count the objects together.

Another idea

You can play another game using Cheerios® on a clean table. Separate the Cheerios® into a few piles of one or two. Ask your child to push the groups with two over to one side of the table and the single Cheerios® to the other side of the table. You can add piles of three or more when he is ready for a challenge.

Let's read together!

Toddler Two
by Anastasia Suen

Color Sorting

You're putting all of the red ones together.

Use two plates and several blocks of two different colors to give your child a chance to sort colors.

Your child will begin to recognize and say color words and sort the blocks by color.

THE
CREATIVE CURRICULUM®
LearningGames®

Why this is important

Knowing color names will enable your child to express herself better. As she practices naming and sorting colors, her understanding and vocabulary will improve. Touching the colored block as she names the color will make it easier to remember the name.

What you do

- Gather together a collection of blocks in two colors. Give her a plate for each color and invite her to sort them. *Can you put the red blocks on this plate and the blue blocks on that plate?*

- Talk about her actions. *I see you put a red block over here. Are you going to find another red block to put with it?*

- Offer help if she does not understand the instructions. *This is a red block. Which plate should we put this red block on?* Help her sort a few blocks until she can do it on her own.

- Add another color to the game when she can successfully sort two colors.

Another idea

Look for other items around your house for your child to sort. When cleaning up toys, ask her to find all the green toys first, then the yellow, etc. Or, let her sort cans in the kitchen by matching up the colors. When folding laundry, your child can help by searching for socks with matching colors. Encourage her to name each color she finds.

Let's read together!

Caps for Sale
by Esphyr Slobodkina

Building Blocks

Show interest when your child plays with blocks by talking about his actions.

With blocks, your child can direct his own play and learn about balance by building with various shapes.

You made three things. Can you tell me about them?

Why this is important

Your child can make decisions and direct his own actions while playing with blocks, and you can observe how he plays on his own. He may not know where to place the blocks at first to balance them, but he will learn quickly if he is allowed to practice. Your child's self-reliance will increase as he learns that he can accomplish what he tries to do.

What you do

- Give your child a box of blocks of various sizes and shapes. Step back and let him explore and experiment on his own. He may form long, flat lines on the floor before stacking the blocks.

- Limit the number of blocks you give your child at first. Discourage him from using the blocks to throw or hit by showing him how he can use them for building.

- Talk about his creations. *You made something with four blocks. Let's count them, one, two, three, four.*

- Invite him to talk about what he builds if he wants to, but let him play quietly if he chooses.

- Provide comfort and understanding if his work collapses before he finishes. *You are really frustrated that your tower fell down.* Encourage him to try again.

Another idea

Use a collection of cans or small cardboard boxes in addition to building blocks. Your child will have more decisions to make about balance as he builds.

Let's read together!

This Is the House That Jack Built
by Simms Taback

Others Have Needs, Too

I need a can opener.

Teach your child how to express her needs by expressing yours.

This helps her understand that others have needs, too.

THE CREATIVE CURRICULUM®
LearningGames®

Why this is important

As your child becomes more aware of her needs, you can help her learn to express them by modeling words that she can someday use. When she begins to understand the needs of others and responds appropriately, your child moves toward having the important ability to listen to others and empathize.

What you do

- Let your child hear you express your needs. Talk in simple terms about what you need, and give her a reasonable way to help. *I need a can opener. Could you get a can opener from the drawer, please?*

- Show appreciation when your child helps you meet a need. *Thank you for helping me when I needed to find my shoes.*

- Help her learn to think about what others need by explaining a situation and asking her about the need. *Here's my bowl of soup. What do I need to eat it with?*

- Ask your child questions about different needs. *It's raining outside. What do I need to keep me dry?*

Another idea

Think of other situations in which your child could help such as riding in the car, visiting a friend, or packing a lunch. *I'm packing a fruit salad in your brother's lunch. What does he need to eat it with?*

Let's read together!

What Do You Need?
by Emanuela Bussolati

Making Os and Xs

You're making a big circle.

Give your child easy, direct experiences in making circles and crossed lines.

Inviting your child to build new shapes with you helps her learn and remember letter-like shapes and forms.

THE
CREATIVE CURRICULUM®
LearningGames®

Why this is important

As your child makes shapes she will begin to see that lines must be closed and curved to be a circle. She will learn to use words that talk about the differences between the straight lines of an *X* and the curved line of an *O*. Practice in distinguishing shapes and symbols prepares her for reading and math later on.

What you do

- Create a circle on the floor with blocks. Invite your child to sit in the middle. Use the word *circle* and help her make her own circles with blocks or other materials.

- Help your child trace the rim of a cup with her finger. Talk about the shape as she traces. *This is a circle. A circle is round like a pizza.*

- Draw big and little circles together using crayons. Your child benefits from the practice even though her circles may be very crooked.

- Take a straight rope and bring the ends together so that it makes a circle.

- Show her how to cross two sticks and to draw a straight line over another straight line to form an *X*.

Another idea

Point to and talk about Xs when you see them in a newspaper or sign. *See the big X on the sign? That's a red X.*

Let's read together!

Stick Kid
by Peter Holwitz

Play With Others

You're rolling the ball back and forth!

Show your child and another child how they can use a ball to play together.

This gives your child a guided experience in cooperating with another child.

What can you make this ball do?

Why this is important

Your child may be ready to begin learning how to play cooperatively with another child. Through cooperative games, she will understand that playing with others can be more fun than competition or solitary play. As she gets older, she will find that many activities can be accomplished only through cooperative behavior. A child who enjoys cooperative games early in life is more likely to approach later situations involving cooperation in a positive way.

What you do

● Show your child and another how to sit on the floor so they can roll a ball back and forth. Stay close to offer help when needed.

● Give them a large towel after they have had time to practice rolling the ball. Invite them to each hold two corners of the towel.

● Place a light ball on the towel.

● Talk about how they can make the ball move. *What happens if you shake the towel? What else can you make the ball do?*

● Use words to explain to them what they are doing. *John, you're holding up your side of the towel so the ball won't roll off. You can make the ball bounce because you're playing together.* If the ball goes astray, help them get it back.

Another idea

Think of other simple games that two children can play together. Encourage them to build with blocks, play with toy cars, or look at books cooperatively.

Let's read together!

A Boy and His Bunny
by Sean Bryan

Choose the Doll's Clothes

You're choosing a pretty gray and white shirt for the girl.

Let your child choose the clothes to put on a paper person while you talk about and ask about the clothing.

Your child can practice making choices about clothing as she learns the words for each item.

Why this is important

Your child will learn the words for the clothing and begin to evaluate choices about what her doll should wear. At first, she may confuse shirts with pants or put them on the wrong parts of the doll, but with practice she will soon understand and begin to say their names. Talking about clothes during the game will help your child become more aware of her own clothing and encourage her interest in dressing herself.

What you do

- Cut out a large paper person and a few simple clothes that will fit over it.

- Invite your child to talk about what clothes the doll might wear.

- Help her choose clothing by asking questions and naming the pieces for her. *I see shoes, pants, a coat, and a shirt. What do you want to put on his feet? Can you find something for him to wear outside so he will be warm?*

- Encourage your child to choose the clothing items and lay them on the doll. After you name them, ask her the name of each piece she chooses. *What are those things called that you're putting on his feet?*

Another idea

Show your child pictures of children in a magazine or catalog. Talk about what they are wearing. *This girl has her warm, winter coat on.* Later, ask your child to explain what the children in the pictures are dressed for such as bedtime, swimming, or cold weather.

Let's read together!

Sweater
by Kit Allen

Drawing Around Things

Your line is going around the can.

Give your child a round plastic cup or objects of other shapes to trace.

Outlining things with his finger or a pencil gives your child practice using the small muscles in his hands as he learns about shapes.

THE CREATIVE CURRICULUM®
LearningGames®

Why this is important

Tracing an object helps your child better understand the relationship of a representation, such as an outline, to an object. With practice, he will become more aware of the differences between the shapes he traces. Using a writing tool, such as a pencil or crayon, helps strengthen his fine motor control (the ability to control the muscles in his hands). Fine motor control is essential to many later skills, such as carefully turning the pages in a book and holding a pencil for writing.

What you do

- Show your child how to hold a box or lid and trace around it with his finger.

- Offer him a pencil or crayon to trace around the shape.

- Follow the line on the paper with your finger. Invite your child to do the same as you talk about the shape on the paper matching the object he traced. *The lid is a circle. You made a circle on the paper when you drew around it with the pencil.*

- Give your child a chance to choose an object to trace. Talk about each shape he chooses.

- Guide his choices toward shapes with simple outlines such as blocks, cups, or plates.

Another idea

Allowing your child to search for new shapes on his own makes him more aware of the shapes of objects around him. Keep many interesting objects handy for him to choose from. Encourage him to trace each new shape and talk about the result on the paper.

Let's read together!

Black on White
by Tana Hoban

Using a Different Voice

Teddy Bear wants to push your car.

Change your voice when you speak to your child.

By varying your voice, you keep her attention and show your child ways to experiment with the tone and volume of her own voice.

Why this is important

Language depends on intonation and rhythm as well as words. One word can have several meanings, depending on the way it is said: "Yes?" (I'm listening), or "Yes" (I agree), or "Yes!" (Hooray!). Your child needs to hear variety in order to create it in her own speech. When she plays whispering games with you, she learns how to control her voice.

What you do

- Speak to your child in a higher or lower voice or whisper in your child's ear. She will pay closer attention to your words when you change your tone, and she may enjoy the novelty of the change.

- Get your child's attention, make her feel special, and show your surprise or delight by changing the tone of your voice. For example, use your lowest bass voice to make her laugh, sing your words to help her relax, or, when she might expect you to call to her from across the room, instead, go to her and whisper.

- Respond to changes in your child's voice by letting her know you understand what she is trying to say. *What a high voice! You sound excited about your truck rolling on the floor!*

Another idea

An easy way to try out new voices is to create a voice for each character in a book you read together. You can give her a chance to choose a voice, or make up new voices and use them each time a character speaks.

Let's read together!

Quiet Loud
by Leslie Patricelli

Happy Face, Sad Face

Happy! This boy looks happy. He's smiling!

Show your child pictures of other people showing their feelings and give him words for how they feel.

Helping him notice the feelings of others develops your child's ability to understand his own emotions.

Why this is important

Seeing feelings expressed on faces around him or in pictures will make it easier for your child to learn the words for those feelings. As he hears other people talk about their feelings, he will begin to see that he can use words instead of actions to express himself. Understanding that others have the same feelings he has helps your child develop his relationships with those around him.

What you do

- Show your child pictures of faces that clearly show an emotion. Talk about the expressions on the faces. *That girl is crying. She looks sad.*

- Encourage him to talk about what makes the people in the pictures have those feelings. Avoid *why* questions because they are harder to answer.

- Ask him if he can remember an event that has made him feel happy, angry, or sad.

- Tell him how you feel. *I feel happy. May I tell you about it?*

- Give him words for his feelings. *I see you look angry. Can you tell me what happened?*

- Comfort him when he cannot express how he feels. He will need your patience and love as he learns to determine what kinds of feelings he has.

Another idea

Talk about the characters in his favorite storybooks and encourage him to tell you what they are laughing or crying about.

Let's read together!

What Shall We Do with the Boo-Hoo Baby?
by Cressida Cowell

Two Together

Here's a board that you can roll a ball down.

Give both your child and a friend a ball to kick or encourage them to roll a ball down a slanting board.

An open-ended opportunity for play with a peer helps your child learn cooperation skills.

Why this is important

When you give two children the chance to have open-ended play together, they can learn to cooperate. Playing with a ball offers your child the chance to practice skills while she learns to play with a peer. Your child will gradually learn how to cooperate first with you, then her peers, and finally larger groups.

What you do

- Give your child a large, soft ball to play with. Show her how to kick it with her toe and encourage her to practice.

- Offer another ball to a child playing nearby. Let the two children play side-by-side.

- Create a cooperative game for the children after they have each had time to play with their own ball. Find a slanted surface for a ball to roll down, such as a long board with one end propped on a box.

- Show the children how to play together. One child stands at the top of the ramp and rolls the ball as the other waits at the bottom to catch it.

- Provide lots of encouragement as they play. *Jeremy, you are waiting so patiently for Michaela to roll the ball to you. Hooray! You caught it. Now you can give it back to Michaela so she can roll it again.*

Another idea

Encourage the children to come up with new ways to use the balls or the ramp together. Step back and allow them to create their own game.

Let's read together!

Is Your Mama a Llama?
by Deborah Guarino

Choosing and Stringing

*I've tied a ring on the end.
Now let's see what you can do.*

Collect a box of things that your child can string on a ribbon or thick piece of yarn.

Your child can practice making choices as she learns to connect objects.

THE
CREATIVE CURRICULUM®
Learning Games®
Copyright 2007 Joseph Sparling

Why this is important

Children develop confidence in themselves when their choices bring them satisfaction. When your child creates a necklace completely on her own, she learns how to play independently and choose for herself. She also practices the skill of using her hands and eyes together to put objects on a string.

What you do

- Fill a box with household objects that have a big hole in them such as curtain rings, large spools, or jar rims. Make sure that the box contains safe objects that allow for independent play.

- Tie a curtain ring (or other large item) at the end of a ribbon and invite her to string other items on, one at a time. Hold the ribbon, if needed, as your child works.

- Talk about the size, color, and feel of the objects. *These rings feel smooth and round. The ribbon is pink and shiny.*

- Help your child wear the finished product as a necklace if she would like to.

- Join your child in hunting for new objects to add to the box. She may notice that jar rims, cookie cutters, or stacking toy rings will work for stringing.

Another idea

Keep the box available so your child can practice stringing when she wants to play again.

Let's read together!

Color Zoo Board Book
by Lois Ehlert

In, Out, and Around

You're under.

Your arms are going through.

My arms are around you.

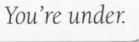

Think of some simple actions to help your child learn position words, such as *in*, *out*, and *under*, and use these words as he plays.

Your child will learn that words not only name objects but can also tell about their positions and relationships.

Why this is important

Understanding that words can tell the positions and relationships of objects is a significant step in your child's language development. Frequently using prepositions—words that show position—will help your child see one object in relation to another or in relation to himself. Relationships help to string words and ideas together in oral and written language.

What you do

- Offer your child a shoebox, a small object, and a large piece of paper. Play a game to show him the meaning of words such as *in*, *out*, and *around*.

- Show him how to put the object in the box and then take it out. He can put the object on top of or under the paper, and he can wrap the paper around the object.

- Place a large box on the floor, so that he can become the object that is *in*, *out of*, and *around* the box. Talk about each position as he plays. *You are in the box. Can you climb out of the box?*

- Use a toy that clearly has a front and a back, such as a small truck. Take turns with your child placing a doll *beside*, *behind*, *in front of*, and *on top of* the truck. Talk about each position.

Another idea

As you care for him and work around your home, use words that help your child understand the position of objects. *Your shirt is in the drawer. Dump the bugs out of the cup. Wrap the towel around your shoulders. Your bear is on the table.*

Let's read together!

Inside, Outside, Upside Down
by Stan Berenstain

Giving One to Each

*One cookie for each plate.
One!*

Give your child just enough napkins, forks, or food items, and let him give one to each person or place at the table.

Setting the table gives your child practical experience with matching one number to one item.

Why this is important

Children like helping with grown-up jobs. Setting the table provides an opportunity for children to practice one-to-one correspondence (one napkin for each plate). The one-to-one relationship is the basis of counting and other math skills.

What you do

- Ask your child to help you set the table.

- Show him how to put a napkin beside one plate.

- Give him just enough napkins and ask him to put one beside each plate.

- Describe what he is doing using the word one. *One for Daddy; one for Grandma; one for Michael.*

- If he no longer has enough napkins to put one at each plate, help him find the place where he put more than one. Explain what happened and offer encouragement. *There were two napkins by this plate. Can you put one at the last plate so each person has one napkin for dinner?*

- Thank your child for helping you set the table.

Let's read together!

One Bear, One Dog
by Paul Stickland

Ready to move on?

After you've done this activity several times with your child, try counting the napkins and places at the table before he starts. This will help him become familiar with the sounds of the number words. *One, two, three, four napkins. One, two, three, four plates. Can you put one napkin at each plate, please?*

A Fun Path

You're following the path.

Talk about your child's actions as he goes along a path of objects by stepping *over*, crawling *under*, jumping *in*, and climbing *on* them.

Your child's physical skills and awareness of space and positional words will increase.

THE
CREATIVE CURRICULUM®
LearningGames®
Copyright 2007 Joseph Sparling

Why this is important

Following an obstacle course encourages your child's physical development as well as his understanding of the position of his body in space. When you use the words that describe his actions as he plays, it is easier for him to learn new vocabulary.

What you do

- Create a path of various obstacles for your child to move through, such as a cardboard box open at both ends, a small stool to climb on and jump off, or a rumpled towel to step over.

- Use a piece of rope or a garden hose as a guide, if needed.

- Change the path occasionally, using new objects each time. Remember your child's skill level and keep the obstacles manageable.

- Stay close by and use position words to talk about what your child does. *You're going under the bench. You're stepping over the paper.*

- Be flexible, allowing your child to step off the path if he chooses. He may strictly follow the sequence or try different obstacles randomly.

Another idea

Invite your child to play "Follow the Leader." Allow him to lead you along the path as he chooses what to do next. You can be the leader and show him a new way to move around each object.

Let's read together!

Jonathan and His Mommy
by Irene Smalls

Words for Time

After your snack, it will be time for a story.

Use words about time such as *before, after,* or *next* when you talk with your child.

Words describing time help her begin to predict when events will happen.

THE
CREATIVE CURRICULUM®
LearningGames®

Why this is important

A child this age has no concept of time as it is defined by hours, weeks, and years. She can only relate time to her actions, such as when the blocks are put away, or to a part of her day that is routine, such as lunchtime. Words about time give your child a tool for sequencing events and predicting what will happen next. Understanding time is important for the literacy skill of recognizing the order of events in a story.

What you do

- Use words that talk about time. *We will eat before we read a story together. After our story it will be time for a bath.* Do not expect your child to understand periods of time. She may recognize what is happening now, a little earlier, or a little later.

- Relate familiar events in her life by using specific language such as *the next time we go to the beach,* instead of *next summer.*

- Use time words throughout the day, such as when you go shopping, make dinner, or visit a friend.

Another idea

When reading a book together, talk about the order of events. After reading a story several times, ask a question such as *Which pig's house did the wolf visit first?* or *What happened after it began to snow?* Your child may respond with simple words or by finding a picture in the book that answers the question.

Let's read together!

A Day With Nellie
by Marthe Jocelyn

Listen and Support

I'm sorry that big dog scared you.

I think you need a hug.

When your child tries to tell you what he needs, listen carefully and provide words to expand what he says.

Your added language and show of sympathy help him feel loved and may help him to express himself the next time.

Why this is important

Listening carefully to what your child says and responding to what he needs let him know he deserves attention. When his needs are met with care, he will become more conscious of the needs of others. Through repetition, he may also learn how to be a good listener.

What you do

- Listen to your child as he begins to express his needs. If necessary, add some words to build on what he says.

- Pay attention to feelings that suggest he has a need that he cannot properly express in words.

- Take his hand and let him guide you when he cannot convey his need with language. Help him use words to express himself. *You did need help with the buggy. I'm glad you came to tell me.*

- Show patience and support as you work to understand his needs.

- Respond to your child's needs with appropriate attention. At times you will act quickly and decisively. At other times you can offer a leisurely, less intense response. Your reaction will help him gauge the importance of his needs.

- Help him think ahead and plan his needs. *What will you need to take with you when you go to Auntie's house?*

Another idea

When your child does use language to express his needs, you may need to interpret his few words. For example, *book* may mean he wants you to read to him. It could also mean his book is out of reach or he might be looking for a specific book. You can reduce his frustration by actively trying to help meet his need.

Let's read together!

The Way I Feel
by Janan Cain

Pair and Sort Pictures

You found one that looks just like mine.

Invite your child to look for a pair in a small group of pictures.

Pairing and sorting helps your child notice similarities and differences.

THE
CREATIVE CURRICULUM®
Learning Games®
Copyright 2007 Joseph Sparling

Why this is important

Playing with sets of pictures gives your child practice sorting and matching pairs by noticing similar parts of pictures. Looking carefully for similarities and differences in the pictures will help him get ready to recognize letters and numbers by their similar or different shapes.

What you do

- Cut identical pictures from two copies of the same magazine, catalog, or advertisement. Make the pictures sturdy by taping each one to a piece of cardboard. Show your child two matching pictures.

- Point out details in one picture and encourage him to find those same characteristics in the other picture. *I have a bird with blue feathers. Can you find another bird that looks like mine?*

- Show three pictures, two of them matching. Invite him to find the pair.

- Mix two sets of pictures and encourage him to look for the two matching pairs.

- Help him get started by holding up a picture and asking, *Can you find one that looks just like this?* Give him the cards to play with as he matches them.

- Add another pair to the game after he matches successfully.

- Invite him to sort the pictures any way he chooses. He may stack them in random piles or find a new way of categorizing them.

Ready to move on?

Hide one picture so the game will end with one odd card. Let him go on a treasure hunt to find the missing picture.

Let's read together!

Dinosaurs Dinosaurs
by Byron Barton

What's Gone?

You've hidden something.

Let's see if I can remember all the toys.

Take away a toy from a group and let your child tell you which one is gone.

Your child will notice things a little more carefully and begin to remember and name something when it is missing.

THE CREATIVE CURRICULUM® LearningGames®
Copyright 2007 Joseph Sparling

Why this is important

In the past, your child may not have had a reason to remember a missing item. Playing this game encourages her to pay attention to her surroundings, and to notice and remember objects. Knowing what is missing is a sign that her memory is developing.

What you do

- Leave two toys on the table or floor during clean-up time.

- Name each item and talk about them. *I see a green ball and a brown teddy bear on the floor.* Invite your child to name the toys.

- Ask your child to close her eyes. Remove one toy while her eyes are shut.

- Invite her to open her eyes and tell you which toy is missing. If she cannot remember, put the item back and play again.

- Give your child a chance to lead the game by hiding a toy for you to notice.

- Add more items to the game as she becomes skilled at noticing the missing object. She may name the absent object before you prompt her.

Another idea

Try to play the game throughout the day: You can purposely give her one sock with two shoes or put out her toothbrush and ask her what is missing. Talk about family members who are not present. *I'm here, you're here; who's gone?*

Let's read together!

Five Little Ducks
by Dan Yaccarino

Cut and Paste

You're making snips with your scissors!

Show your child how to make small cuts in a strip of paper or around the edge of a larger sheet.

Cutting with scissors provides a great way to have fun while creatively improving eye-hand coordination.

Why this is important

When a child can use his fingers and wrists well, he can begin to use scissors. Your child will improve his skill in using his fingers and hands through experience with scissors. Children need to know how to use the basic tools of their culture. He will need to know how to use scissors throughout his life, and the fine motor control he develops will be helpful when he begins writing.

What you do

- Offer your child safe, children's scissors, and sit with him as he uses them.

- Let him hold the scissors in a way that is comfortable for him.

- With another pair, show him how the blades open and shut.

- Help him by holding a thin strip of firm paper and letting him snip it. He may cut all the way across the strip and split it into pieces, or he may cut small snips in the edge.

- Offer positive feedback for his efforts. *You cut a lot of snips in the edge of the paper! You're cutting very carefully.*

- Allow him to try to hold the paper as he cuts, but offer more help if needed.

Another idea

Demonstrate how to put paste on the scraps of cut paper and stick them to a larger piece of paper. Let him explore the paste with his fingers.

Let's read together!

Alphabet House
by Nancy Elizabeth Wallace

Help Him Help Himself

You're pouring carefully.

Allow your child to serve himself at meals from bowls or containers that are small or are not full.

Your child will increase his independence as you give him opportunities to do things for himself.

You're putting three carrots on your plate.

Why this is important

By arranging food and utensils so that he can serve himself, you allow your child to make simple choices about the food he adds to his plate. This also allows him to complete a task independently.

What you do

- Put food on the table in small bowls with large spoons. If you need to use a large bowl, make sure that it is not very full.

- Invite your child to serve his own plate. Show him how to use the serving spoon. Provide a small plastic pitcher and cup so that he can pour his own drink. Be sure to place all items within his reach.

- Guide his choices about which foods to take and how much to add to his plate. Encourage him to eat a smaller amount at first and to take more later if he still wants it. *I see you put three small carrots on your plate. After you eat them, you can have more if you like.*

- Expect a small mess with each attempt. As his skill develops, he will be able to serve his food more neatly.

Let's read together!

The Carrot Seed
by Ruth Krauss

Another idea

Letting your child serve himself is not appropriate all the time. The needs of the entire family determine which mealtimes will be most convenient for this learning experience. Let your child help plan meals that will work best for practicing his new skills. Talk about healthy food choices as you plan, prepare, and eat each meal together.

What Would Happen If...?

Do shoes go on first?

Create some silly situations from daily life for your child to figure out.

Your child will understand a little more about the logic of familiar routines and in what order things must happen.

Noooo, socks.

Why this is important

Your child may now be able to use her imagination to understand make-believe situations. By asking her *What would happen if …* questions, she may begin to notice and understand what must happen first in a situation and to think about logical order. Recognizing the necessary order or sequence in which events happen helps with reasoning, problem solving, and understanding the plot in a story.

What you do

- Create situations that present time or space in an incorrect order and share them with your child. Pretend to make mistakes when doing simple tasks. For example, you can zip her coat before she puts her arm in the sleeve, or hold her glass upside down as you start to tip the milk carton to pour.

- Ask her, *What would happen if… you put on your shoes and then put on your socks?* Or ask, *What if you got in the bath and then we took off your clothes?*

- Give your child time to answer with words or gestures to show the proper order of events.

- Repeat her words in a full sentence. For example, if she says all wet. You might say, *You're right. Your clothes would get all wet!*

- Listen every day for the words *first, then, next,* and *until.*

- Encourage her when you hear them in her speech. *Yes! We do need to get a plate first!*

Ready to move on?

Encourage your child to make up a few silly situations for you to solve. Challenge her by offering a few wrong answers for her to correct.

Let's read together!

Blue Hat, Green Hat
by Sandra Boynton

Run and Walk Together

Let's run!

Talk about what is happening as you and your child run fast, walk slowly, gallop like a horse, or shuffle like an elephant.

Your child will learn words at the same time he learns to coordinate his body and control his actions.

Why this is important

Playing outside provides an opportunity for your child to develop his skills in running and moving. When you talk about each motion, you help him learn the words for his actions. Becoming aware of his body movements is an important first step in forming an intentional plan about how to move and when. Moving quickly from running to walking makes him aware of his body and how to direct it.

What you do

- Go outside with your child and show him a few special ways of moving.

- Exaggerate your walking steps and say, *Look at me walking.*

- Start to run as you say, *Now I am running.*

- Take your child's hand and repeat the motions with him.

- Use the words *run* and *walk* as you perform the action so that your child will remember the difference between the words.

- Encourage your child to invent some special ways of moving such as running in a circle, galloping like a horse, running in circles, or walking very slowly.

- Listen for the words *run*, *walk*, *fast*, and *slow* in your child's speech. Offer an encouraging response when he uses them. *You're right, Jeremiah. We walk inside and run outside.*

Another idea

Let your child lead in a game of "Follow the Leader." Encourage him to try new ways of moving such as walking backwards or walking sideways.

Let's read together!

Run, Jump, Whiz, Splash
by Vera Rosenberry

Tell Family Stories

Show me what Latisha does.

Mama says, "Let's play Hide-and-Seek."

We'll pretend these are our family.

Let your child move stick puppets to act out a family story that she and you tell together.

Telling stories will help your child understand the relationships among people in families.

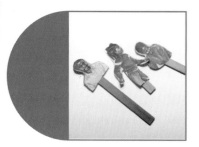

Why this is important

Handling the puppets helps your child to see her family as a group. Playing with the family puppets may help her to see herself as an important part of a family. She can use her place in the group and her knowledge about her family members to make up stories using familiar information. Having an understanding of how stories are made will later help her better understand the stories she reads.

What you do

- Collect some pictures of family members and friends to cut up.

- Glue the pictures to popsicle sticks to make puppets.

- Make up a story about the family. Encourage your child to move the puppets around to act out the story.

- Include a few real events along with imaginary events in your story.

- Ask your child questions to involve her in making up part of the story. *What do you think she did next? How did it make you feel?*

- Talk about the adults so that your child can be aware of them as people with feelings and needs.

- Encourage her to tell her own story with the puppets.

Another idea

Show your child pictures of herself as a baby and answer her questions about her life then. Talk and ask about people in daily events, such as going to the supermarket. *Who sat in the grocery cart? Which friend did we see there? Who put the groceries in the bag?*

Let's read together!

On the Night You Were Born
by Nancy Tillman

I See Something That Is...

Give two clues, one about color and one about the object's use, to help your child find an object.

Your child will notice more than one thing about a familiar article.

I see something red, and you can read a story from it.

You're looking carefully…

You found it!

CREATIVE CURRICULUM®
LearningGames®

Why this is important

Considering two features of an object requires your child to do a two-step evaluation to identify it. He must also listen to your directions in order to determine the important information. Weighing both parts of your description will help him come to a conclusion as he will do with many evaluations throughout his life.

What you do

- Invite your child to play a simple version of *I Spy* with you.

- Give two hints. The first hint should be about the color of the object and the second should be about the object's use. *I spy something blue. You drink from it.*

- Play the game by facing the general direction of the object. Ask your child to touch the object when he sees it.

- Respond positively to his accomplishment. *Yes, that cup is blue. You can drink from it. You listened very carefully!*

- Repeat the clues if your child chooses incorrectly and offer encouragement. *You're right. That is blue. Now can you find something blue that you can drink from?*

- If you need to, make the game easier by placing three items in front of your child and ask for one of the objects using the same two clues.

Another idea

Keep this game in mind when you are waiting in the doctor's office, visiting relatives, or any place your child needs extra attention. Be sure to choose objects your child can point to, touch, or bring to you.

Let's read together!

Hush! A Thai Lullaby
by Mingfo Ho